CALIFORNIA
MISSIONS

Discovering Mission San Fernando Rey de España

BY OSCAR CANTILLO

Cavendish
Square

New York

Published in 2015 by Cavendish Square Publishing, LLC
243 5th Avenue, Suite 136, New York, NY 10016

Copyright © 2015 by Cavendish Square Publishing, LLC

First Edition

Website: cavendishsq.com

This publication represents the opinions and views of the author based on his or her personal experience, knowledge, and research. The information in this book serves as a general guide only. The author and publisher have used their best efforts in preparing this book and disclaim liability rising directly or indirectly from the use and application of this book.

CPSIA Compliance Information: Batch #WS14CSQ

All websites were available and accurate when this book was sent to press.

Library of Congress Cataloging-in-Publication Data

Cantillo, Oscar.
Discovering Mission San Fernando Rey de España / Oscar Cantillo.
pages cm. – (California missions)
Includes index.
ISBN 978-1-62713-106-3 (hardcover) ISBN 978-1-62713-108-7 (ebook)
1. San Fernando, Rey de España (Mission : San Fernando, Calif.)—History—Juvenile literature. 2. Spanish mission buildings—California—San Fernando Region—History—Juvenile literature. 3. Franciscans—California—San Fernando Region—History—Juvenile literature. 4. Gabrielino Indians—Missions—California—San Fernando Region—Juvenile literature. 5. Chumash Indians—Missions—California—San Fernando Region—Juvenile literature. 6. California—History—To 1846—Juvenile literature. I. Title.

F869.S26C37 2014
979.4'93—dc23

2014010504

Editorial Director: Dean Miller
Editor: Kristen Susienka
Copy Editor: Cynthia Roby
Art Director: Jeffrey Talbot
Designer: Douglas Brooks
Photo Researcher: J8 Media
Production Manager: Jennifer Ryder-Talbot
Production Editor: David McNamara

The photographs in this book are used by permission and through the courtesy of: Cover photo by Mariusz S. Jurgielewicz/Shutterstock.com; © Richard Wong/Alamy, 1; © Richard Wong/Alamy, 4; © Kayte Deioma, 9; © Kayte Deioma, 10; RES Photo Services, 11; © 2014 Pentacle Press, 13; Nheyob/File:Mission San Carlos Borromeo de Carmelo (Carmel, CA) - Mora Chapel, cenotaph - Fray Fermín Lasuén.jpg/Wikimedia Commons, 15; © Pentacle Press, 16; Henry Chapman Ford/File:Mission San Fernando LACMA M.79.53.5.jpg/Wikimedia Commons, 20–21; Courtesy of UC Berkeley, Bancroft Library, 22; Photo courtesy of Rev. Raymond A. Bucko, S.J. Ph. D., 23; Detroit Publishing Co./File:Mission San Fernando Postcard, circa 1900.jpg/Wikimedia Commons, 24–25; © Pentacle Press, 26; Courtesy of UC Berkeley, Bancroft Library, 31; Alex Covarrubias/File:Flag of Mexico.svg/Wikimedia Commons, 33; Mike Quach/File:Brand Park 10.JPG/Wikimedia Commons, 34; Courtesy CMRC, 36; Kayno919/File:San fernando mission.jpg/Wikimedia Commons, 41.

Printed in the United States of America

Contents

Mission San Fernando Rey de España was
one of the most successful missions.

4

1
The
Spanish Arrive

Situated on busy Mission Boulevard, twenty-five miles outside the city of Los Angeles, stands a cream building with an orange-tiled roof. This is Mission San Fernando Rey de España, the seventeenth of twenty-one missions, or religious communities, built along California's coast between 1769 and 1823. Founded in 1797 by a man named Fray Fermín Francisco de Lasuén and named after Saint Ferdinand, who was king of Spain over 500 years earlier, this mission met with much success during its existence.

EL CAMINO REAL

Mission San Fernando Rey de España also became known to travelers on *El Camino Real*, meaning "The Royal Highway." This was the main road that went up and down **Alta California**— today known as California—linking the missions together. Many travelers stayed there, exchanging news with the **friars**, or *frays* in Spanish, who ministered to the Native population and the people of the *pueblo*, or settlement, of Los Angeles. El Camino Real made it easy for people to travel from one mission to the other. Each mission was about a day's ride apart. Over time many settlers journeyed on El Camino Real to make new lives in the area.

SPANISH SETTLE ALTA CALIFORNIA

Over two centuries before Mission San Fernando Rey de España was established, Europeans began exploring the Americas. Colonists from England, France, and the Netherlands built settlements there. However, by 1536, Spain's overseas empire, called New Spain, was the largest, and included present-day Mexico (called **Baja**, or "lower," **California**), the Antilles, the Philippines, Central America, half of South America, and much of the western United States.

Yet, before 1769, no Spanish settlements had been built in *Alta*, or "upper," California. Until then, very little was known about this large territory. Explorers such as Juan Rodríguez Cabrillo and Sebastián Vizcaíno had searched along the coast and set up ports. However, since there was no water route between the Atlantic and Pacific oceans, and no riches like Hernán Cortés had found when he claimed New Spain in the 1500s, Spain was not interested in sending settlers there.

In 1767, King Carlos III of Spain heard that the Russians and the English were interested in settling the land. They had already explored Alaska and the upper west coast and built settlements there, and now they were moving farther south. King Carlos III realized that Alta California was too important for Spain to lose, so he and the Spanish government decided that a chain of missions would be set up along the coast of Alta California. Spanish friars would settle there, with soldiers at *presidios*, or military forts, nearby. It was the soldiers' job to protect the missions, and the friars' job to **convert** the Native people into Spanish citizens.

2
The Tongva and the Chumash

Prior to Europeans settling the Americas, thousands of **indigenous people** populated the land. They set up communities, called tribes, spoke their own languages, and lived simply. The Native group most associated with Mission San Fernando Rey de España was the Tongva, however, the populous Chumash were also involved with the mission.

WHERE THE NATIVE PEOPLE LIVED

The original name of the Tongva people has been lost over the centuries. In the mission era, they were known as Gabrieleños or Fernandeños, depending on which mission was closer to their village. Today, they prefer the name Tongva, and in 1994 they were officially recognized as an indigenous Native community.

The Tongva lived around present-day Los Angeles, on the Channel Islands, and on Santa Catalina Island. They spoke different dialects of *Shoshone*, an ancient Native language that originated in the tribes of Nevada. They lived in either small villages or larger settlements. The larger settlements could hold up to 200 people who stayed in one place year round. The smaller villages were nomadic, meaning the people moved from place to place every season to search for food. The Chumash lived to the north of the Tongva, mostly in the area that is now Ventura County. There were five or six times as many Chumash as there were Tongva. Both lived off the land, finding food in the ocean such as salmon, clams, and sharks; and some in the forest, such as deer. Acorns, berries, and roots from the ground were also important food sources.

THEIR WAY OF LIFE

The Chumash and Tongva had many things in common. Groups were led by a council of elders, who passed down traditions from generation to generation. Music and dance were important parts of their daily and spiritual lives. They played musical instruments and sang songs for harvesting, hunting, warfare, and births.

The houses of the Chumash and Tongva were shaped like domes. The frames of the houses were made of wooden poles or whale ribs. Over this frame hung brush and willow branches, which formed the roof and sides of the dwelling. Each usually had a fire pit and a hole in the roof so that smoke could escape. Several families could live in one of these houses, though the smaller homes built by the Tongva in their smaller villages usually held only one family.

Both groups used resources around them to make weapons, tools, and clothing. The Tongva were skilled in weaving Native women's hats and sandals, and making bowls from stone and arrowheads from minerals such as serpentine. The Chumash made beautiful baskets, and mortars and pestles used for cooking

The Tongva and Chumash made boats out of reeds and trees. This is a model of a Tongva canoe called a ti'at.

or grinding seeds. Both groups made their own canoes to travel on the water. The Tongva had three kinds of boats, all different sizes and made of different materials. The Chumash made *tomols*, or large canoes, that could hold up to ten people. Bathing was particularly important to the Tongva, and they were required to do so every day.

Both groups drew paintings on the walls of caves to tell the stories of their way of life. They used rocks, berries, and minerals to create different colors.

RELIGIOUS PRACTICES AND BELIEFS

Both the Tongva and the Chumash had their own gods and believed all life had spirits. Religious ceremonies were held in special buildings—which the Tongva called *yuva'r*—and led by

Descendants of the Tongva tribe continue their ancient traditions today.

a **shaman**. The Chumash also had astronomers who would study the sky before making important decisions. Some tribes, such as the Chumash, buried their dead, but the Tongva **cremated** theirs.

CLOTHING

Because the climate in the area was mild, in warmer weather men and children often wore little or no clothing. The women wore skirts made from branches, reeds, and grasses. In colder months, they wore capes made of warm animal fur.

All of this changed when the Spanish missionaries arrived in the 1700s. Whole cultures were then transformed forever.

3
The
Mission System

Even before Spain's decision in 1767, the mission system had been used for centuries as a way of settling an area. Spanish missionaries were sent around the world to convert people to Catholicism, a branch of Christianity that followed the teachings of Jesus Christ. The people they encountered would learn Spanish traditions and become Spanish citizens.

FRAY JUNÍPERO SERRA

The man who led the first group of missionaries to Alta California was Fray Junípero Serra, whom historians now recognize as the father of the California missions. Born in Majorca, Spain, he joined the **Franciscan order** at the age of sixteen. He went on to convert many Native people in Baja California, and his success and dedication to his faith led

Fray Junípero Serra is known as the first leader of the California missions.

to his becoming the first president of the California missions. In his lifetime, Fray Serra founded nine of the twenty-one California missions. The man who founded Mission San Fernando Rey de España was Fray Serra's successor, Fray Lasuén.

THE GOAL OF THE MISSIONARIES

From the Catholic Church's point of view, the main goal of the missions was to convert the local people to Christianity and turn them into productive, tax-paying Spanish citizens. They also wanted the Natives to help build the missions' many buildings and farm the land.

The Spanish did not understand the Native peoples' beliefs or lifestyle and thought they lived sinful lives as **pagans**. They believed it was their duty to bring them to Christianity and to teach them how to live "civilized" lives. Every newly converted person was called a **neophyte**.

HOW THE MISSIONS WERE BUILT

The California missions were built about a day's ride apart from each other on the best farming land available. The Spanish missionaries did not see the land as their own, however. They believed that once the Native people had learned the Christian way of life, and had taken on the responsibilities of Spanish citizenship, the land could be returned to them. The Spanish thought this would take no more than ten years, but it didn't turn out that way. In the end, the Native tribes lost most of their land—and much of their culture.

REASONS FOR JOINING

Many Native people joined the missions for shelter, a steady food supply, and the opportunity to learn new skills. However, they did not realize how great an effect the missions would have on their once-vibrant cultures, or their very lives. In order to become part of the religious community of the missions, a person had to give up their cultural, religious, and even physical freedom. Forced to work for long hours under a strict schedule, many suffered under the control of the soldiers and the friars.

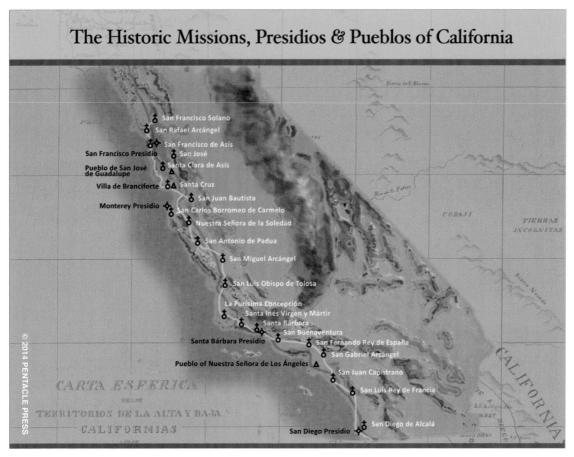

The Historic Missions, Presidios & Pueblos of California

San Francisco Solano
San Rafael Arcángel
San Francisco de Asís
San Francisco Presidio
San José
Pueblo de San José de Guadalupe
Santa Clara de Asís
Villa de Branciforte
Santa Cruz
San Juan Bautista
Monterey Presidio
San Carlos Borromeo de Carmelo
Nuestra Señora de la Soledad
San Antonio de Padua
San Miguel Arcángel
San Luis Obispo de Tolosa
La Purísima Concepción
Santa Inés Virgen y Mártir
Santa Bárbara
Santa Bárbara Presidio
San Buenaventura
San Fernando Rey de España
San Gabriel Arcángel
Pueblo of Nuestra Señora de Los Ángeles
San Juan Capistrano
San Luis Rey de Francia
San Diego de Alcalá
San Diego Presidio

In all, twenty-one missions lined California's coast connected by El Camino Real (indicated by the yellow line on the map). All were guarded by four presidios.

4
Founding the Mission

By the time Fray Lasuén decided in 1797 to build Mission San Fernando Rey de España, the Alta California mission system had been operating with some success for almost thirty years. In fact, the location of this newest mission on the California coast had been chosen nearly three decades earlier.

SELECTING THE SITE

Fray Serra and the Spanish government of New Spain agreed in 1768 to build the first Alta California mission, San Diego de Alcalá. In 1769, Spanish explorer Gaspar de Portolá, Fray Serra, and his colleague Fray Juan Crespí made their way over land to San Diego to found the mission. During their journey, they passed through a valley, which they named *La Valle de Santa Catarina de Bononia de Los Encinos* (The Valley of St. Catherine of Bononia of the Oaks). The Native people knew this area as Achois Comihabit. While exploring the valley, the group stopped one night to make camp.

Fray Crespí wrote in his diary that many local Tongva people came to visit the camp that night. Each person brought food as a gift to the Spaniards, and in return, the Spaniards gave them beads and ribbons. It was also noted in Fray Crespí's diary that he and Fray Serra both felt this area would make a good spot for a future mission, due to the welcoming nature of the Native people and the four springs that provided water for drinking and farming. The land around this area was also rich in nutrients and appropriate for developing a mission.

This statue of Fray Lasuén sits at Mission San Carlos Borroméo.

However, it was not until 1797 that Fray Lasuén would decide that the time was right to return and found Mission San Fernando Rey de España in La Valle de Santa Catarina de Bononia de Los Encinos. The mission would be situated on land between Mission San Gabriel and Mission San Buenaventura, making travel easier from mission to mission. And, as Fray Crespí had predicted in his diary nearly thirty years earlier, Mission San Fernando Rey de España would see great success in food production and the conversion of the Native people.

THE BEGINNINGS OF THE MISSION

The spot that Fray Lasuén picked for the seventeenth mission was on land that had been granted to Francisco Reyes, mayor of the pueblo of Los Angeles. Fray Lasuén was interested in starting the mission on some of Reyes' grazing fields. Although Reyes fought to keep the land, he eventually gave it up to the missionaries in his last year as mayor. Later, he became godfather to the first child **baptized** at the mission.

THE MISSION AND THE TONGVA

Before the land for Mission San Fernando Rey de España had been bought by the Catholic Church, the Tongva had lived in the area for many decades. Even before Fray Lasuén arrived, the mission system itself had played an ongoing role in their lives. Mission San Gabriel Arcángel had been built twenty-six years earlier, in 1771, and had greatly changed the way the Tongva there lived. The Native groups living in the San Fernando Valley had also been impacted by diseases brought by the Spanish when they first came to this part of the world. Several hundred Tongva lost their lives during terrible epidemics that spread around the coastal

Many Native people thought the only way to rid themselves of diseases was to be baptized into the religion of the Spanish, who were not affected by illnesses.

groups. Some Tongva had lost their faith in their shaman and way of life, and for this reason, some treated the arrival of Fray Lasuén and the new mission as a blessing. It was a way for the Natives to survive, as the mission would provide many comforts and learning opportunities.

DEDICATING THE MISSION

On September 8, 1797, Fray Lasuén dedicated Mission San Fernando Rey de España in honor of Saint Ferdinand. A few missionaries and neophytes arrived from Missions Santa Bárbara and San Buenaventura to celebrate the new mission, so a *ramada*, or refuge made of branches, was built to shelter the celebrants. The neophyte musicians brought their instruments to perform Christian songs and chants they had learned. On that day, ten Native children were baptized.

LEADING THE MISSION

Fray Lasuén left Francisco Dumetz from Mission San Buenaventura and Fray Juan Lupe Cortés from Mission San Gabriel Arcángel to take charge of the new mission at San Fernando. Their first task was to begin work on the mission's buildings. Soon after dedicating Mission San Fernando Rey de España, the missionaries and soldiers built simple living quarters, a temporary church, and a storeroom. In keeping with tradition, nearby missions sent livestock, such as cattle and sheep, and seeds to help the new mission grow. However, it would take more people to build the entire mission.

5
Early Days at the Mission

Mission San Fernando Rey de España was one of the largest missions in the mission system. Within the first two months of its dedication, the friars had baptized many neophytes who came to live and work at the mission. It became a popular mission for the Tongva people to join, and it continued to grow over the years.

BUILDING CONTINUES

By November 1797, the first permanent structure had been built: a small chapel made of adobe—sun-dried bricks made of straw, mud, and manure. The Spanish used adobe because it kept cool in the summer and warm in the winter, making it a good building material for the missions. Around the same time, a **granary**, a weaving room, and a storeroom were added.

Almost a year after construction on the mission began, Fray Cortés left. However, the other friars there continued to have success instructing and converting the Tongva, and the mission community grew very quickly. By 1799, the chapel was too small to fit the growing number of neophytes and had to be rebuilt. Other mission buildings also had to be enlarged. The neophytes, under the direction of the friars and soldiers, would continue to expand or repair the buildings as needed in the years to come. By the time the mission's last building, the Long Building, was completed in 1822, it was said that if all the buildings were lined up, they would span a full mile (1.6 kilometers).

Separate houses to the east and west of the mission were built for neophyte families, forming a village. As the number of neophytes grew over the years, little adobe houses were added to this village. A cemetery was also created nearby. This would be the final resting place of many neophytes, including Espiritu Chijulla Leonis, the daughter of Chumash chief Oden. She had been born and educated at Mission San Fernando Rey de España.

THE SHAPE OF THE MISSION

Traditionally, missions were designed as a quadrangle, a four-sided enclosure around which the mission buildings stood. In 1802, a building was raised that completed the quadrangle of Mission San Fernando Rey de España. It housed a storeroom, a carpenter shop, and granaries.

In 1806, a third permanent church was completed. This large church measured 185 feet (56 meters) by 35 feet (11 m). The church walls appear to lean outward, as they were built five feet (1.5 m) thick at the base and only three feet (0.9 m) thick at the top. A staircase on one side of the chapel led up to the two-story bell tower, where three arched openings held the mission's three bells. A large fountain and basin were built in the courtyard. The neophytes used their artistic talents to paint the mission walls with images of flowers, vines, seashells, and animals.

THE FRIARS' QUARTERS

In most of the missions, the church was connected to the *convento*, the friars' living quarters. However, the convento at Mission San Fernando Rey de España was a later addition—not begun until 1810—so it was built apart from the quadrangle. (Before the convento was built, the friars lived in a ranch house once belonging to Don Francisco Reyes.) The convento was two stories tall, and while primarily used as the priests' dormitory, this large space also served as a guesthouse that welcomed many visitors over the years—particularly the terminally ill. In 1813, a small building for *majordomos* was added. Majordomos were

European settlers who lived at the mission and supervised Native American workforces. A beautiful corridor with nineteen Roman arches would eventually connect the convento to the church.

So many visitors traveling on El Camino Real came to Mission San Fernando Rey de España that the friars decided to add more guest rooms to the convento. Several rooms were added over a period of twelve years, until the convento became the largest building of all the missions. It became known as the Long Building. When it was completed, it contained more than twenty rooms, including a reception room, kitchen, storehouse, winery, refectory or dining hall, and chapel.

San Fernando Rey de España, pictured in this late nineteenth-century etching by Henry Chapman Ford, grew quickly.

SUCCESSFUL CROPS

Mission San Fernando Rey de España was well known for its excellent wines and olive oil. The mission community, aided by the warm climate, grew over 32,000 grapevines and 70 acres (28 hectares) of olive trees in orchards outside the mission walls. The neophytes collected the olives and grapes and crushed them to make these **commodities**. In addition, crops such as wheat, corn, barley, and chickpeas were also grown by the neophytes.

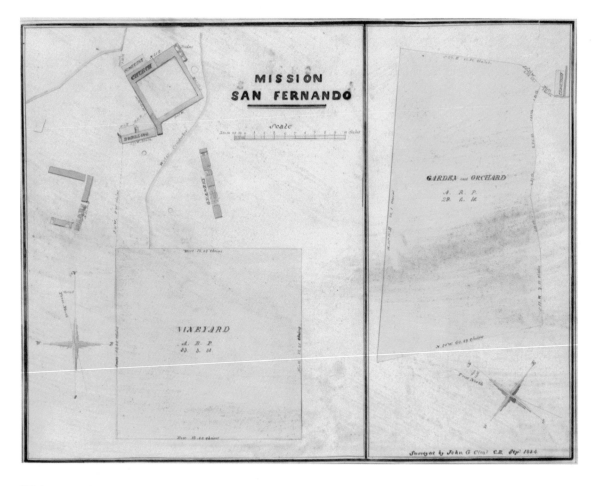

This map from 1854 shows the mission's layout. Vineyards, gardens, and orchards took up much of the land.

6
Everyday Life at the Mission

Day-to-day life varied little at the missions. Each mission had a strict work and prayer schedule for the neophytes, soldiers, and friars that differed from what the neophytes had experienced prior to joining the mission system.

BELLS

At Mission San Fernando Rey de España, as at other missions, the chapel bells played an important role in daily life. They were used to signal to the mission community to wake, to sleep, to work, and to eat. Of the original four bells used at Mission San Fernando Rey de España during its existence, two still remain: one in the belfry (or bell tower), and another inside the mission complex. This latter bell dates back to 1796 and is thought to have been given to the mission by a Russian count who arrived

This bell has been part of the mission for over 200 years.

Once completed, the Long Building became a place where many people worked daily.

there in 1806. The bell has inscriptions of the mission and of a Russian Orthodox Church official engraved into it.

THE DAILY SCHEDULE

During a typical day at the mission, the workers usually woke around sunrise and made their way to the chapel. Everyone, except the sick, attended Mass, the main religious ceremony. Sometimes a neophyte who had been taught by the friars would lead the prayers, which were recited in the local language as well as in Spanish.

After Mass, everyone ate breakfast. Small children ate with their parents at home in the village. The older boys ate in the community kitchen, and the girls eleven years and older ate in the *monjerío*, the living quarters for unmarried girls. Everyone drank hot chocolate and ate *atole*, a type of porridge made from cooked corn. Around

8 a.m., children went to church for religious classes taught by the friars, while everyone else began their chores.

Between 11 a.m. and 2 p.m., a midday meal of *atole* might be served with mutton—the meat from a full-grown sheep—or beans. *Tortillas*, flat cakes made of ground meal, were also served. Work stopped after lunch for a *siesta*, an afternoon rest or nap, and began again around 4 p.m.

At sunset, the day's work was finished and everyone met again at the church for prayers. Dinner usually consisted of *atole* or *pozole*, a porridge made with meat and vegetables. After dinner, the neophytes were given a brief amount of free time to relax and enjoy playing games. Women went to sleep at 8 p.m., while the men went to sleep at 9 p.m.

Many Saturdays were spent working. On Sundays and holidays, however, everyone was allowed to rest and play after a few hours

Female neophytes made food at all twenty-one missions, including grinding corn.

of prayer. The Catholic Church has many holidays for its patron saints, which the friars referred to as holy days.

WORK DIVIDED

Neophytes learned different skills from the friars—farming, taking care of livestock, and how to weave on large looms—and practiced these skills every day during long hours of work.

At Mission San Fernando Rey de España, men and women performed different tasks. The men usually spent the day working in the fields, tending to livestock, or building mission structures. They herded the cattle, horses, and sheep. Wheat, barley, peas, beans, corn, figs, and peaches were grown. When harvest season ended, they made adobe bricks from soil mixed with water and straw or made tiles from clay.

The women weaved the cloth used at the mission, as well as blankets, sheets, tablecloths, towels, and napkins. They also prepared food, cleaned, and washed clothing and other items for all of the people at the mission.

The neophytes also produced the wine for which the mission became famous. They climbed into large barrels filled with ripe grapes and stomped on them until the juices ran out of the barrel through special wooden pipes. At the peak of its wine production, Mission San Fernando Rey de España produced 2,000 gallons (7,570.8 liters) of wine and 2,000 gallons (7,570.8 L) of brandy each year.

A DIFFERENT LIFESTYLE

The life the neophytes lived at the missions was very different from what they'd known in their tribes. Living among nature, they had worked extremely hard for a brief period of time and then rested. At the mission, however, they were forced to work long hours without rest. They also had to give up almost every part of their culture and beliefs. Before long, many neophytes missed their old way of life and tried to escape, but were usually caught, brought back, and severely punished. When asked why they had run away, many said they had felt as if they were in jail.

Today, we realize it is important to respect other people and cultures. Just because a culture may be different doesn't mean that it is better or worse than others. Although the mission system brought new skills to the Native Californians, in many ways it robbed them of their culture and freedom.

7
Challenging Times

Mission San Fernando Rey de España was one of the most successful missions in Alta California. Almost from its inception it attracted neophytes, and over the decades that followed, its location on the busy road near the growing city of Los Angeles made it a good place for travelers to stop for the night. In 1811, the mission reached its peak with over 1,000 neophytes having converted and joined the mission community. Most of the mission buildings had been built, and crop production was also high. This was a time of success for the California missions, and Mission San Fernando Rey de España was one of the leaders. However, this era of growth could not last forever.

THE WAR WITH MEXICO

In 1810, New Spain became divided by war. Those settlers who were loyal to the Spanish crown wanted to remain part of the empire. However, there were also many settlers who were unhappy with the way Spain governed the New Spain territory and wanted it to become its own independent country, called Mexico.

The war lasted for eleven years and greatly affected the mission system. Those people in support of an independent

Mexico blocked off supply routes. This prevented Spain from sending supplies to the missions, as they had done in the past. The friars were forced to trade with British and American trade ships to get the supplies they needed.

When the Spanish government stopped paying wages to the soldiers stationed at the nearby presidios, they demanded food and other supplies from the missions instead of planting food to help themselves. As time wore on and these soldiers became more frustrated and angry, they treated the neophytes and Native people with increasing cruelty. As a result, more and more neophytes fled the missions.

The community at Mission San Fernando Rey de España struggled to supply the soldiers with food, clothing, and weapons. The friars were even forced to pay the soldiers' wages by giving them supplies from their annual stipends!

CONFRONTATION

The friar in charge of Mission San Fernando Rey de España at that time was Fray José Antonio Urrestí. He and the other missionaries ran the mission's day-to-day activities and converted many people to Christianity. In 1810, however, they were faced with an unexpected conflict. Native people from the Mojave tribe arrived at nearby San Gabriel's mission lands and stole sheep and other materials valuable to the mission. They next planned to attack San Gabriel Arcángel and Mission San Fernando Rey de España. When the Mojave were stopped by soldiers from the Santa Barbara presidio, they began targeting violent attacks against the

Native groups that lived around the missions and traded with the friars.

DECLINING NUMBERS

Even before the Mojave attacks began, the Native community at Mission San Fernando Rey de España was already shrinking from other causes. Many of the Native people died from European diseases such as mumps, chicken pox, and the flu when epidemics swept over the California mission system in the early 1800s. The neophytes living in the missions and the Natives in the surrounding areas had never been exposed to these diseases before the Europeans came, and therefore had not developed immunity to them.

NATURAL DISASTERS

From 1811 to 1815, the San Fernando Valley experienced other disasters that affected Mission San Fernando Rey de España. In 1811, a flood in the Los Angeles area alarmed the community and destroyed many crops. Soon after, in 1812, an earthquake rocked the mission, damaging some buildings. The church was especially affected, and more support was added to the ceiling and walls to protect it against other earthquakes in the area over the coming years. Another flood threatened the area in 1815. This flood greatly harmed the *pueblo* of Los Angeles, twenty-five miles away. There was so much debris in the Los Angeles River that it created its own dam, changing the course of the river itself.

STARVATION

By the 1820s, the best years of Mission San Fernando Rey de España were behind it. The living situation for those at the mission did not improve. Many of the mission's crops were ruined by insects and wild animals that year. Caterpillars ate the bean crops, locusts destroyed the wheat fields, and rabbits and worms ruined the corn. The harvests were no longer large enough to feed so many people. Despite this, the soldiers insisted that the friars provide them with the supplies they needed. Fray Francisco Ibarra, who was in charge of Mission San Fernando Rey de España in 1820, wrote many letters to the commander of the troops complaining of the starvation that the neophytes and other missionaries suffered because of the soldiers' demands.

Then Mexico won its independence from Spain in 1821—and the mission system changed forever.

In the mid-1820s, life at the mission was difficult. The mission system was about to undergo a radical transformation.

8
Secularization

After 1821, the new government of Mexico wanted people to settle farms and towns on the land in Alta California. In the 1830s, Mexican officials passed laws to **secularize** the missions. These laws allowed the Mexican government to take the control of the missions away from the Franciscan friars, which provided more settlers the opportunity to own land in the region.

SECULARIZING MISSION SAN FERNANDO REY DE ESPAÑA

Under these new laws, the missions would be run by the Mexican government instead of the Catholic Church. The mission communities would become towns, and the mission churches would be led by priests who did not do missionary work. All the neophytes would be free to leave the missions.

It was not until 1834 that Governor José Figueroa officially secularized Mission San Fernando Rey de España. A plan was made to divide the land between settlers and neophytes. However, many settlers were greedy when it came to dividing the fertile farmlands, and the officials in charge of carrying out the plan were corrupt. Furthermore, the Native people did not understand the concept of land ownership. For them, owning a piece of land was like owing a piece of sky!

Many of the neophytes did not want to be farmers. Some went

back to their mountain villages. Others went to work at ranches near the mission for little more than room and board. They were not treated much better than they had been at the mission, and often, they were treated worse. Many of the ex-neophytes never learned to be self-sufficient outside the mission.

Mexico gained independence in 1821 and became its own country.

Mexico's plan to reorganize Alta California included sending all Spanish-born friars back to Spain. However, they allowed Fray Ibarra to stay and continue to run Mission San Fernando Rey de España. In 1835, however, Fray Ibarra decided to leave on his own. He did not want to continue watching the decline of the mission. The remaining friars struggled to continue their work, and Mission San Fernando Rey de España continued to operate until 1845.

LIFE AFTER SECULARIZATION

In 1842, the first discovery of gold in California occurred not far from the mission. It brought many people searching for the valuable mineral. Some people became so desperate that they dug up parts of the mission itself, hoping to find gold underneath.

Mexico's possession of California didn't last for long. In the 1840s, the United States decided they wanted the land of Alta California as their own. The Mexican–American War began. In 1848, America won and Alta California, renamed California, became part of the United States in 1850.

Throughout the 1900s, Mission San Fernando was slowly restored.

9
The Mission Today

Today, Mission San Fernando Rey de España still stands in Los Angeles. It is a testament to the mission system's influence on the state's history. Over the years, however, earthquakes and vandalism badly damaged it. In 1916, restoration efforts to bring it back to its original state began. In 1974, the Roman Catholic Archdiocese of Los Angeles decided to build an exact replica of the original church. Efforts to restore it were halted after an earthquake in 1994 but continued in 1996.

MISSION POPULARITY

Thanks to its carefully preserved beauty and proximity to Hollywood, the picturesque area surrounding Mission San Fernando Rey de España has been featured as a location in many movies, including *Back to the Future*, *E.T.*, and *Star Trek*. The mission is also a popular tourist destination. Visitors to the Long Building can still see the huge wine press, smoke room, and refectory.

The convento now houses one of the oldest libraries in California, which includes books collected by the friars. This collection, which was once put in storage, had to be completely restored before being permanently housed here. The gardens have also been brought back to their former glory. The mission's original fountain still stands, but was moved 300 feet (91 m) from its first location.

A beautiful park now exists across the street from this historic landmark. At its entrance stands a statue of Fray Serra, with his arms around a Native American boy. Fray Serra continues to be a man remembered for his role in bringing the missions to California.

MISSION LEGACY

Today, Mission San Fernando Rey de España is a reminder of the triumphs and trials of the mission period. The Spanish who settled the area forever changed the culture and way of life for many Native people. They also shaped the history of California, and developed crops and harvesting techniques that contributed to its success over the centuries.

Today the mission is known for its beautiful gardens, its library, and its history.

10
Make Your Own Mission Model

To make your own model of the San Fernando Rey de España mission, you will need:

- Foam Core board
- paint (cream, black, red, green)
- uncooked lasagna noodles
- cardboard
- miniature flowers/trees
- floral foam blocks
- glue gun sticks
- pins
- tongue depressors
- toothpicks
- scissors
- ruler

DIRECTIONS

Adult supervision is suggested.

Step 1: Use a piece of Foam Core board that is 20" × 20" (50 cm × 50 cm) for your mission base. Paint it with the cream-colored paint, and let dry.

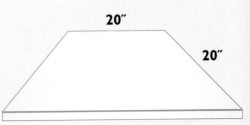

Step 2: Cut out four pieces of floral foam that are 8" × 3" (20 cm × 8 cm) and paint with the cream-colored paint. Let dry.

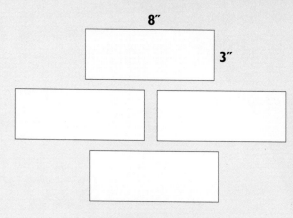

Step 3: Cut out two pieces from the floral foam that are 3" × 3" (8 cm × 8 cm) and 5" × 3" (13 cm × 8 cm). Paint with the cream-colored paint. Let dry.

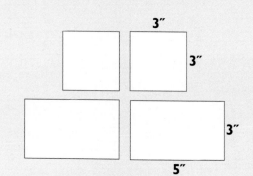

Step 4: Use pins to attach four floral foam blocks that are 8" × 3" (20 cm × 8 cm) to form a box shape. Place on mission base.

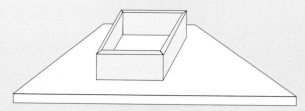

Step 5: Attach two pieces of floral foam that are 3" × 3" (8 cm × 8 cm) and 5" × 3" (13 cm × 8 cm) to the top of the mission front.

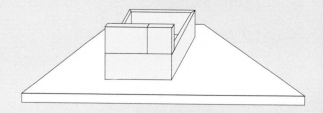

Step 6: Take lasagna pieces and break them through the wide part into two pieces that are 3"(8 cm) long and three pieces that are 5"(13 cm) long. Paint all pieces red and set aside.

Step 7: Cut two tongue depressors in half through the wide part and paint them black. Set aside.

Step 8: To make roofs, cut out two cardboard pieces that are 6"× 2" (15 cm × 5 cm). Bend each in half. Pin one to each side of the church front.

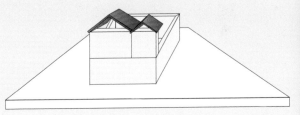

Step 9: Cut a piece of cardboard to measure 5"× 3"(13 cm × 8 cm). This will be for a terrace roof to the right and front of the church.

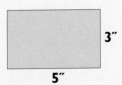

3"

5"

Step 10: To make the columns for the terrace roof, glue three glue gun sticks to the base on the right, front side of the church as shown.

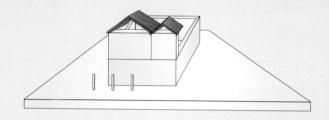

Step 11: Cut out a piece of cardboard that is 5" × 3" (13 cm x 8 cm). Glue a cardboard piece on top of columns at a slant. Glue one 5" (13 cm) piece of lasagna on top of the terrace roof.

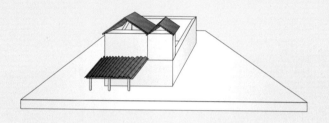

Step 12: Glue red lasagna pieces that are 3" (8 cm) long to the 3" (8 cm) church roofs. Glue the two pieces that are 5" (13 cm) long onto the 5" (13 cm) church roofs.

Step 13: Glue black tongue depressors onto the front of the church for windows. Glue one tongue depressor onto the left front side to make a doorway.

Step 14: Form a cross with toothpicks and attach to the top of the church building.

Step 15: Decorate with miniature flowers and trees.

The model of San Fernando Rey de España when completed.

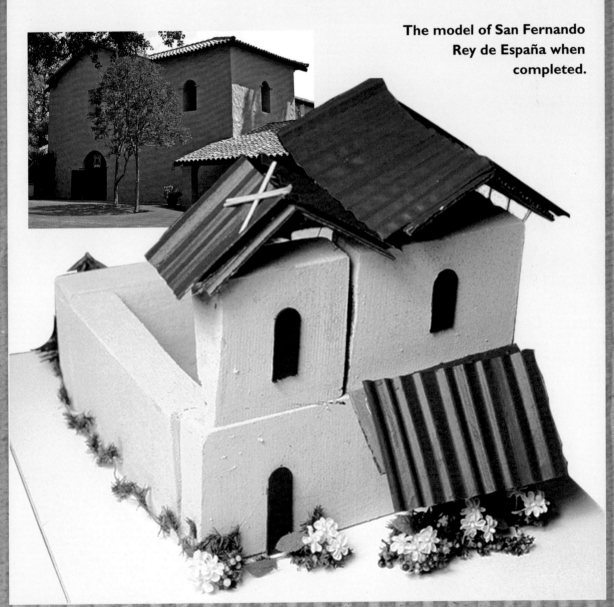

Key Dates in Mission History

1492	Christopher Columbus reaches the West Indies
1542	Cabrillo's expedition to California
1602	Sebastián Vizcaíno sails to California
1713	Fray Junípero Serra is born
1769	Founding of San Diego de Alcalá
1770	Founding of San Carlos Borroméo del Río Carmelo
1771	Founding of San Antonio de Padua and San Gabriel Arcángel
1772	Founding of San Luis Obispo de Tolosa
1775–76	Founding of San Juan Capistrano
1776	Founding of San Francisco de Asís
1776	Declaration of Independence is signed

1777	Founding of Santa Clara de Asís
1782	Founding of San Buenaventura
1784	Fray Serra dies
1786	Founding of Santa Bárbara
1787	Founding of La Purísima Concepción
1791	Founding of Santa Cruz and Nuestra Señora de la Soledad
1797	Founding of San José, San Juan Bautista, San Miguel Arcángel, and San Fernando Rey de España
1798	Founding of San Luis Rey de Francia
1804	Founding of Santa Inés
1817	Founding of San Rafael Arcángel
1823	Founding of San Francisco Solano
1833	Mexico passes Secularization Act
1848	Gold found in northern California
1850	California becomes the thirty-first state

Glossary

Alta California (AL-tuh KA-luh-for-nyuh) The mission area today known as the state of California.

Baja California (BAH-ha KA-luh-for-nyuh) The Mexican peninsula directly south of the state of California.

baptize (BAP-tize) To perform a ceremony of baptism which makes someone a member of a specific Christian church.

commodity (kuh-MOD-ih-tee) An object that is special or valuable to a person or a group of people.

convert (kun-VURT) To change religious beliefs.

cremate (KREE-mayt) To reduce to ashes by burning.

Franciscan order (fran-SIS-kin OR-der) A communal Roman Catholic order of friars, or "brothers," who follow the teachings and example of Saint Francis of Assisi, who did much work as a missionary.

friar (FRY-ur) A brother in a communal religious order. Friars can also be priests.

granary (GRAH-na-ree) A windowless building used for storing grain.

indigenous people (in-DIJ-en-us PEA-pel) People native born to a particular region or environment.

neophyte (NEE-oh-fyt) The name for an indigenous person baptized into the Christian faith.

pagans (PAY-gen) People holding religious beliefs other than those considered "main world" religions.

secularize (seh-kyoo-lur-rize) A process by which the mission lands were made to be nonreligious.

shaman (SHAH-min) A religious and spiritual leader who heals the sick through medicine and ritual.

Pronunciation Guide

atole (ah-tol-ay)

Chumash (CHOO-mahsh)

convento (kahn-BEN-toh)

El Camino Real (EL kah-MEE-noh RAY-al)

monjerío (mohn-hayr-EE-oh)

pueblos (PWAY-blohs)

Shoshone (show-SHOW-nee)

siesta (see-EHS-tah)

tomol (TOH-mul)

Find Out More

To learn more about the California missions, check out these books and websites:

BOOKS

Duffield, Katy S. *California History for Kids*. Chicago, IL: Chicago Review Press, 2012.

Gibson, Karen Bush. *Native American History for Kids*. Chicago, IL: Chicago Review Press, 2010.

Leffingwell, Randy, and Alastair Worden. *California Missions and Presidios*. St. Paul, MN: Voyageur Press, 2005.

Williams, Jack S. *The Tongva of California*. New York, NY: Rosen Publishing, 2003.

Young, Stanley, Melba Levick, and Sally B. Woodbridge. *The Missions of California*. San Francisco, CA: Chronicle Books, 2004.

WEBSITES

California Mission Foundation
www.californiamissionfoundation.org
Find quick and easy facts about the missions and discover more about the organization that preserves and protects the missions today.

California Missions Online
www.californiamissionsonline.com/missions
Discover information on specific missions, including photos, history, and mission models.

California Missions Resource Center
www.missionscalifornia.com
Interact with a mission timeline, videos, and photo gallery and unlock key facts about each mission in the California mission system.

Official Websites of the Tongva and Tataviam Native Groups
www.tongvapeople.org and www.tataviam-nsn.us
Learn more about the Native people who lived at Mission San Fernando Rey de España, their history, and how they live today by visiting these websites.

Index